UK employme_

CW00394215

Staff Handbooks

Bullet Points

email: robin@worklaw.co.uk
website: www.worklaw.co.uk
telephone: 07549 168 675

ISBN: 9798622408120
Imprint: Independently published

UK Employment Law

Bullet Point Booklets

published

to be published shortly

Disclaimer

This series of booklets is titled *UK employment law*. This is not an entirely accurate title. The laws of England and Wales are the same. The laws of Scotland and Northern Ireland, so far as they relate to employment law, are broadly the same as in England and Wales but may differ occasionally. This booklet indicates if laws differ significantly.

Employment law is complex and changes frequently due to political, social and economic pressures, and the law might have changed by the time you read this booklet: the publication date is on the title page.

Please view this booklet as a brief, *bullet-pointed* guide to employment law. It is not a complete guide. You must not rely on this booklet for anything other than a brief overview of the law and procedures: our attempt to simplify the law might cause misunderstanding and ambiguities.

This booklet does not—and cannot—cover everything. For example, where bullet-point lists are given they may be incomplete as only more common items might be listed.

You are advised to consult a specialist in employment law to answer specific questions.

Staff Handbooks

A staff handbook may be called many things. For example,
- an employee handbook;
- a staff manual.

For the purposes of this booklet we will call the document a *handbook*.

The law does not require an employer to have a handbook; so why have one?

The answer is because those employment terms which are *non-contractual* can be put in a handbook.

Basically, a handbook should comprise the *rules and regulations* for the *day to day running* of the business; whereas, an employment contract should comprise the binding terms and conditions under which an employee works.

A binding contract between two parties may be changed only if both parties agree to the proposed change: this is the basic principle of contract law.

An employment contract (as the name suggests) is a contract like any other.

So, if an employer needs to change a term in an employment contract the employee has to agree to the change otherwise the employer will be in breach of contract (and at risk of claims to an employment tribunal or a court).

A fundamental concept in an employment tribunal is that the parties (employer and employee) should behave *fairly* towards each other (hence, *unfair* dismissal claims). However, in a court (as opposed to in an employment tribunal) the concept of fairness is largely disregarded and mostly what matters is whether there has been a breach of the contract.

A *breach of contract claim* may be made in an employment tribunal, under certain circumstances, and such claims are treated the same way as they would be in a court. In other words, the concept of fairness is largely disregarded and the employment judge focuses on the wording of the document in dispute.

Handbooks need to be drafted carefully: the wrong word, a missing word, or a word out of place, can mean that the judge regards a clause in a handbook as contractual when the employer intended that it should be non-contractual.

If it is made clear when a term in the handbook is non-contractual, the employer may change that term, within reason, even though the employee objects. But we emphasise the words 'within reason': an act (or omission to act) by an employer should not impact adversely on an employee unless justified.
So it makes sense for the employer to keep the contents of an employment contract to the minimum (that is, put into the contract only those matters which the employer is required by law to include), and put everything else in a handbook.
It is difficult to change employment contracts; not so difficult to change handbooks.

To reiterate, the contents of an employment contract are *contractual* and the contents of a handbook should be—in so far as is possible —*non-contractual*.

Before examining what should be included in a handbook, we need to look at what must be included in a written statement pursuant to s.1 Employment Rights Act 1996 (as amended).

A Written statement

The law does not require an employer to give an employee a *written* employment contract.

However, the law does require the employer to give the employee *a document* containing certain mandatory information.

The document we are referring to has no set-name in law, but is called various names such as;
- a written statement of employment particulars;
- a written statement;
- particulars of employment;
- and variations on the above or other names.

Lawyers sometimes refer to the documents as a *section one statement* because the obligation to give the document arises from sec.1 Employment Rights Act 1996.

For the purposes of this booklet, we will call the document *a written statement*.

This document is not, in itself, an employment contract, but is merely evidence of what the terms and conditions of employment probably are.

The reason the document is not an employment contract is because an unwritten (or partly written) employment contract arises as soon as one person agrees to work for another, even though there may be nothing in writing (or not everything in writing) as to the terms and conditions of the employment.

An unwritten employment contract might consist of a combination of:
- some unspoken, but implied terms;
- some unspoken terms imposed by law;

- some unspoken terms imposed by *custom and practice*;
- some agreed terms not put in writing
- some agreed terms in writing.

By *unspoken* we mean that the relevant terms have not been discussed but are deemed to exist in an employment contract. An example of an *implied term* which is deemed to exist in every employment contract (written, unwritten or part-written) is the implied term of *mutual trust and confidence*. Basically, it is implied in every employment contract that the employer and the employee should have trust and/or confidence in each other to carry out their mutual obligations under the employment contract, and neither should behave in such a way as to damage that trust and confidence.

An example of a term *imposed by law* would be an obligation on the part of the employer to provide a safe system of work.

An example of *custom and practice* could be the payment of overtime at a specific percentage increase on the normal hourly rate over a lengthy period of time even though there is nothing in writing about this.

Changes effective on 6th April 2020

Currently, the law says that an employer must give employees a written statement within 2 months of the start of employment, if their employment contract lasts at least a month or more.

However, the law will change: on and after the 6th April 2020 all new employees and also *workers* will have the right to be give a written statement on or before their first day of employment.

A person is generally classed as a *worker* if they have a contract to do work or provide services *personally*, and only have a limited right to subcontract the work.

Mandatory information

We now need to look at what a written statement must contain by law.

The information required by section 1 Employment Rights Act 1996 (as amended) to be included in the written statement is as follows (we quote the wording of the Act):

(1) Where an employee begins employment with an employer, the employer shall give to the employee a written statement of particulars of employment.

(2) The statement may be given in instalments and (whether or not given in instalments) shall be given not later than 2 months after the beginning of the employment (please remember that paragraph (2) of the legislation will change on the 6th April 2020: the written statement will have to be given on the first day and not within 2 months).

(3) The statement shall contain particulars of—

(a) the names of the employer and employee,

(b) the date when the employment began, and

(c) the date on which the employee's period of continuous employment began (taking into account any employment with a previous employer which counts towards that period).

(4) The statement shall also contain particulars, as at a specified date not more than 7 days before the statement (or the instalment containing them) is given, of—

(a) the scale or rate of remuneration or the method of calculating remuneration,

(b) the intervals at which remuneration is paid (that is, weekly, monthly or other specified intervals),

(c) any terms and conditions relating to hours of work (including any terms and conditions relating to normal working hours),

(d) any terms and conditions relating to any of the following—

(i) entitlement to holidays, including public holidays, and holiday pay (the particulars given being sufficient to enable the employee's entitlement, including any entitlement to accrued holiday pay on the termination of employment, to be precisely calculated),

(ii) incapacity for work due to sickness or injury, including any provision for sick pay, and

(iii) pensions and pension schemes,

(e) the length of notice which the employee is obliged to give and entitled to receive to terminate his contract of employment,

(f) the title of the job which the employee is employed to do or a brief description of the work for which he is employed,

(g) where the employment is not intended to be permanent, the period for which it is expected to continue or, if it is for a fixed term, the date when it is to end,

(h) either the place of work or, where the employee is required or permitted to work at various places, an indication of that and of the address of the employer,

(j) any collective agreements which directly affect the terms and conditions of the employment including, where the employer is not a party, the persons by whom they were made, and

(k) where the employee is required to work outside the United Kingdom for a period of more than one month—

(i) the period for which he is to work outside the United Kingdom,

(ii) the currency in which remuneration is to be paid while he is working outside the United Kingdom,

(iii) any additional remuneration payable to him, and any benefits to be provided to or in respect of him, by reason of his being required to work outside the United Kingdom, and

(iv) any terms and conditions relating to his return to the United Kingdom.

Not all the above information need be given in the same document, and may be given in instalments, but for the purposes of this booklet we will assume that all the information is given in a single written statement.

As we will see later in this booklet, the information required by section 1 is referred to in the sample handbook under the heading PART A (contractual).

Handbook contents

Worklaw has produced a sample handbook, an editable copy of which is available to download for free from https://worklaw.co.uk/staffhandbook.php.

It is unlikely that all of the sample handbook as worded will be suitable for your particular business and you will need to check that specific details in the sample draft are relevant to you, and amend the draft accordingly. For example, if you run a catering business you will need specific clauses relating to food hygiene and food allergies (these clauses are not in the sample handbook).

Worklaw's sample handbook is divided into:
An Introduction;
Part A, which is expressed to be contractual;
Part B which is expressed to be non-contractual;
A reference to stand-alone essential Policy documents.

Part A of the sample handbook

The Introduction to the handbook states:

Part A is contractual, that is to say, the matters referred to in Part A form part of your Employment Contract. The Company reserves the right to review, revise, amend or replace the content of your Employment Contract and this Staff Handbook and introduce new terms and conditions and new policies from time to time or to vary existing terms and conditions and/or policies to reflect the changing needs of the business and to comply with new legislation.

Obviously, you should amend Worklaw's draft handbook in accordance with the specific requirements of your particular business, but you are advised not to change the wording above. The wording is copied from the wording of the handbook in a case called Bateman & Ors v Asda Stores Ltd. Asda's handbook included the following wording:

'The Company reserves the right to review, revise, amend or

replace the content of this handbook, and introduce new policies from time to time to reflect the changing needs of the business...'. The essential words are *"The Company reserves the right to review, revise, amend or replace the content of this Handbook"*. In fact, the Asda handbook did not include the words *your employment contract*, which Worklaw has added.

Relying on the wording in their handbook (referred to above), Asda varied some terms in employment contracts and employees claimed that Asda's power to vary contracts was limited to non-contractual terms. However, the Employment Appeal Tribunal ruled that Asda, by unambiguously including a clause in the handbook stating that it could unilaterally change terms and conditions without the consent of the employees, were entitled to do as they did.

A few words of caution: although the employer reserves a right to vary employment contracts unilaterally the employer must not act in such a way as to breach an implied term which is deemed by law to exist in every employment contract, and which is usually called by lawyers *the implied term of trust and confidence* (an analysis of this term is beyond the scope of this booklet).

Also, an employment tribunal or a court could reach a decision which conflicts with, or overturns the Asda-case. Sometimes, different judges reach different judgments in cases which are seemingly similar as to their facts.

Basically, the wording in a contract or a handbook may be challenged in an employment tribunal or in a court. Words are always open to interpretation depending on their context and background. There is no certainty that an employment tribunal or a court would find that Worklaw's added wording (*'the content of your Employment Contract'*) would entitle an employer to vary an employment contract, as opposed to a handbook (but it may do).

To sum up (in lawyer 'speak'), the general position is that contracts of employment can only be varied by agreement. However, in the employment field an employer, or for that matter an employee, can reserve the ability to change a particular aspect of the contract unilaterally by notifying the other party as part of the contract that this is the situation. However, clear language is required to reserve to one party an unusual power of this sort.

We now need to explain why Part A is expressed to be *contractual*, when we have said that, in so far as is possible, a handbook should be expressed to be non-contractual.

Part A is said to be contractual

Worklaw takes the view that the mandatory information, which must be included in a written statement, is likely to be regarded as contractual by an employment tribunal or a court, when referred to in a handbook, even when the employer says that it is non-contractual or uses the word *discretionary* as a qualifier. We emphasise the word 'likely' because there is no certainty about this: in 'lawyer speak' each case is examined on its own merits. But Worklaw takes the view that the following terms in Part A are likely to be regarded by a judge as contractual even if expressed to be non-contractual, so Part A makes clear that you, as the employer, agree that these terms are contractual.

PROBATIONARY PERIOD

Under current law, it is not necessary for a written statement to refer to a probationary period. However, on and after the 6th April 2020 it will be necessary to say whether or not the employment is subject to probation, and if so, give details of any probationary conditions and their duration.

JOB DUTIES

An employer needs to be flexible, hence the wording: *You may be asked to undertake other duties that fall within your capabilities.* However, as always, an employer must be mindful of the implied term of mutual trust and confidence, referred to in the preceding section, and not act in such a way so as to be in breach of this implied term.

PLACE OF WORK

The right to vary the place of work will very much depend on the job in question and what is reasonable in the circumstances.

WORKING HOURS

The right to vary working hours will very much depend on the job in question and what is reasonable in the circumstances. And, employers need to be aware and mindful of the Working Time regulations which impose certain limits on hours of work. Also, the terms and conditions relating to *overtime*, if any, should be made clear and unambiguous.

PAY

Employers must be careful to ensure that they pay at least the national minimum wage and are advised to read Worklaw's booklet: The National Minimum Wage. Also, employers should be mindful that a failure to pay wages on time could amount to a fundamental breach of the employment contract.

LAY-OFFs and SHORT-TIME WORKING

Strictly speaking, it is not necessary to refer to 'lay-offs' or short-time working. However, unless the employer has reserved a contractual right to lay-off employees or place them on short-time working the employer will be in breach of contract if the employer does either.

HOLIDAYS

Worklaw has a draft sample employment contract available to download for free from https://worklaw.co.uk/employmentcontracts.php which includes some 18 subclauses relating to holidays. But if your business has additional rules relating to, say, booking holidays, they can be set out in the handbook; either in Part A if the term is contractual or in Part B if the term is non-contractual.

SICKNESS

Worklaw's sample employment includes some 21 subclauses relating to SSP, but if your business has, say, terms relating to *contractual* sick pay (as an addition to, or as an alternative to *statutory* sick pay) these contractual terms can be included in Part A of the handbook. However, if sick pay (over and above SSP) is *discretionary* then these discretionary terms should be included in Part B of the handbook which is *non-contractual*.

DEDUCTIONS FROM PAY

Although this clause is in the handbook, employers who wish to reserve the right to deduct money owed by the employee to the employer from wages should ensure that the employee signs a document to authorise the deduction otherwise, in the absence of the employee's signature, any purported right to make deductions will be unenforceable in law. The best policy is to draft a stand-alone document relating to the specific deduction(s) and obtain the employee's signature to that document.

WORKERS UNDER 18

Under the Working Time regulations, special rules apply to employees under 18 as to limits on their hours of work, which includes a 30 minute rest break if they work more than 4.5 hours; daily rest of 12 hours and weekly rest of 48 hours.

PREGNANCY AND OTHER STATUTORY RIGHTS

Employees have statutory rights concerning the following matters:
Maternity leave
Parental leave
Time-off for dependents
Paternity leave
Adoption leave
Shared parental leave
And flexible working.
Worklaw advises that an employee's rights regarding the matters, listed above, should be set out in separate stand-alone policy documents and the relevant document given to the employee when

applicable. Some draft stand-alone policies can be downloaded from Worklaw's website for free at https://worklaw.co.uk/staffhandbook.php : the policies are listed under Part C (Statutory policies).

Later in 2020, in addition to the statutory rights listed above, bereaved parents will have the right to 2 weeks of leave following the loss of child under the age of 18, or a stillbirth after 24 weeks of pregnancy.

NOTICE

The minimum notice to terminate employment an employee is entitled to by law is one week for each complete year worked up to 12 once they have been employed for a month. The minimum notice an employee is required to give their employee is one week once they have been employed for a month. The statutory notice an employee is required to give their employer remains at one week throughout their employment. Therefore, most employment contracts stipulate that the parties should give each other longer notice; for example, a month, to terminate employment.

An employer should reserve a right to make a payment in lieu of notice, otherwise, doing so will be a technical breach of contract.

GARDEN LEAVE

'Garden leave' is when an employee remains employed during the duration of the notice period but is not required to do any work. Usually, such a clause only applies to senior managers, when the notice period is one of several months, possibly to stop them working for a competitor during those months.

RIGHT TO WORK IN THE UK

It goes without saying that that all employees must have the legal right to work in the UK. Employers who employ illegal workers (even inadvertently) are liable to criminal prosecution and/or very heavy financial penalties, so we think a reference to 'the right to work in the UK' should be number 1 on the list in Part A.

Part B of the sample handbook

Part B is expressed to be non-*contractual*. The Introduction to the handbook states:

Part B is non-contractual, that is to say, the matters referred to in Part B are policies, procedures and work practices with which you must comply for the efficient day to day running of the business. Part B does not form part of your Employment Contract and may be replaced, withdrawn or varied by the Company, in whole or in part, at any time.

Hence, an employer has wider scope to change Part B, which is expressed to be non-contractual, when compared to Part A which is expressed to be contractual.

However, the same words of warning, as were given above in relation to Part A regarding the implied term of mutual trust and confidence, also apply to Part B.

For ease of reference, we repeat the paragraph as follows: *although the employer reserves a right to vary employment contracts unilaterally the employer must not act in such a way as to breach an implied term which is deemed by law to exist in every employment contract, and which is usually called by lawyers the implied term of trust and confidence.*

Worklaw's sample handbook contains some 90 clauses, some of which will not be relevant to your business, and your business is likely to need some additional clauses.

But probably every business needs clauses in their handbook relating to the following

INDUCTION
PERSONAL DETAILS
PERSONAL DATA
TRAINING
APPRAISALS
IMPROVEMENT
TIMEKEEPING

DRESS CODE
OTHER EMPLOYMENT
ABSENCES FROM WORK
MEDICAL APPOINTMENTS
MEDICAL EXAMINATIONS
JURY SERVICE
ATTENDING COURT
BAD WEATHER
SAFETY AT WORK
ACCIDENTS AT WORK
FIRST AID
FIRE DRILL
BOMB ALERTS
NO SMOKING POLICY
ENVIRONMENTAL RESPONSIBILITY
DRUGS AND ALCOHOL
CONFIDENTIALITY
EQUAL OPPORTUNITIES
BULLYING and HARASSMENT
COMPANY PROPERTY
EMPLOYEE'S PROPERTY
RIGHT TO SEARCH
SIGNING IN AND OUT
PUBLIC DUTIES
FORCES RESERVIST
RELIGIOUS HOLIDAYS
COMPASSIONATE LEAVE
PROTECTIVE CLOTHING AND EQUIPMENT
DATA PROTECTION
REFERENCES
'OPEN DOOR' POLICY
TRADES UNION
CHANGES TO HANDBOOK

HEALTH and SAFETY

REDUNDANCY

The following clauses are probably necessary for office staff:

BONUSES

EXPENSES

COMPUTERS and INTERNET

SOCIAL MEDIA

COMPANY MOBILE TELEPHONES

PERSONAL TELEPHONE CALLS

Businesses employing drivers will probably need clauses relating to the following:

OWN MOTOR VEHICLES ON COMPANY BUSINESS

COMPANY MOTOR VEHICLES

COMMERCIAL VEHICLES

The following are some suggested miscellaneous clauses:

STOCK and CASH

EXPENDITURE

SECURITY OF PREMISES

CCTV MONITORING

ID PASSES

VISITORS

WHISTLEBLOWING

BRIBERY

CONFLICT OF INTERESTS

CRIMINAL CONVICTIONS

NOTICE BOARDS / INTRANET

PRESS ENQUIRIES

INTELLECTUAL PROPERTY

RETIREMENT

RECOUPMENT RELATING TO ABSENCES

HOME WORKING

Employers will also need:

A GRIEVANCE PROCEDURE and

A DISCIPLINARY PROCEDURE

The advice is usually to include the wording of the grievance procedure in a written statement or employment contract, and to refer to the disciplinary procedure in the same written statement or employment contract, but include the wording of the disciplinary procedure in a separate document such as the handbook.

Most of the above clauses are included in Worklaw's sample handbook which you can download for free from https://worklaw.co.uk/staffhandbook.php.

Written policies

An employer should also have the following written policies, either in separate (stand-alone) documents or included in another document such as the handbook.

It is usually more practical to refer to the the existence of these policies in a written statement or an employment contract or in the handboook, and then have the full wording in a separate document which can be given to an employee as and when relevant and needed.

The following written policies relate to statutory rights which must be given to employees if they are relevant:

MATERNITY

PATERNITY

PARENTAL LEAVE

ADOPTION

SHARED PARENTAL LEAVE

BEREAVEMENT

FLEXIBLE WORKING

Although the following matters are referred to briefly in the sample handbook, it might be sensible for an employer to have a separate stand-alone policy in respect of each:

BRIBERY

EQUAL OPPORTUNITIES

DATA PROTECTION

WHISTLEBLOWING

CARS

INTERNET

The above list is not exhaustive: depending on your

business you might need additional policy documents.

Sample handbook

The handbook (with index and policies) is available for free on Worklaw's website at https://worklaw.co.uk/staffhandbook.php and, for your ease of reference, is also printed below (except for the index and policies). Please read Worklaw's booklet entitled Disciplinary Procedures for advice on grievance procedures and disciplinary procedures (these procedures are not included in the sample handbook which is printed below).

If you use the sample handbook (in whole or in part) in your business, you do so at your own risk. Please remember that it was not drafted specifically for your business and may not be entirely suitable and some clauses might be inappropriate or counter-productive. Worklaw can draft a staff handbook specifically for your business for £297 including policy documents.

STAFF HANDBOOK

INTRODUCTION

This Staff Handbook is divided into Part A and Part B.

Part A is contractual, that is to say, the matters referred to in Part A form part of your Employment Contract. The Company reserves the right to review, revise, amend or replace the content of your Employment Contract and this Staff Handbook and introduce new terms and conditions and new policies from time to time or to vary existing terms and conditions and/or policies to reflect the changing needs of the business and to comply with new legislation.

Part B is non-contractual, that is to say, the matters referred to in Part B are policies, procedures and work practices with which you must comply for the efficient day to day running of the business. Part B does not form part of your Employment Contract and may be replaced, withdrawn or varied by the Company, in whole or in part, at any time.

You are expected to familiarise yourself with both Parts A and B of this Handbook. If you require clarification regarding any part of this Handbook please ask your line manager.

A reference to your 'line manager or 'senior member of management' includes any other member of the Company with authority to give you instructions. Failure to follow such instructions without reasonable cause will be a disciplinary matter. The reference to your 'Employment Contract' is a reference to the document you were given at the commencement of your employment with the Company which sets out the terms and conditions of your employment as required by section 1 of the Employment Rights Act 1996.

In addition to your Employment Contract you might have been give a letter, which we refer to as a 'Job Offer Letter, setting out any additional terms of employment relevant to your particular employment; not all staff receive a Job Offer letter.

This Handbook should be read in conjunction with any other written terms and conditions of employment you receive.

There may be policies and procedures or work rules with which you must comply in addition to those set out in this Handbook. Your line manager will inform you of these additional policies, procedures or rules.

You will be notified of changes to this Handbook by a general notice to all employees affected by the change.

If practical, you will be given at least a week's notice in writing of any significant changes which may be given by way of an individual notice or a general notice to all employees.

Changes will be deemed to be accepted by you unless you notify your line manager or a senior member of management of any objection you have in writing as soon as possible. If you have a reasonable objection you can also raise the matter using the Company's Grievance Procedure.

For the avoidance of doubt, in the event of an inconsistency between what is written in your Employment Contract and what is written in the Staff Handbook it is the Employment Contract which applies.

In your own interests, please retain all documentation issued to you relating to your employment with the Company.

PART A

As stated in the Introduction, Part A is contractual.

1. RIGHT TO WORK IN THE UK

1.1 The Company is required to confirm that all employees have the legal right to work in the United Kingdom, before they can start work with the Company.

1.2. You will need to provide the Company with proof of your eligibility to work in the UK. You should bring your passport or birth certificate or work permit (if applicable), or other relevant documentation with you on your first day. A copy of the document or documents will be made by the Company and the copy will be kept in your file in the office. Your employment is subject to your producing the relevant documents.

1.3. If you are unsure about your status, then please ask your line manager who will be able to advise you.

1.4. Your contract of employment will be terminated immediately without notice should you lose, at any stage of your employment, the right to work in the UK.

1.5. It will be your responsibility to ensure that you obtain the required permissions and proof of status that we require in order to comply with UK legislation. If you fail to do this then we will have to terminate your employment immediately.

2. PROBATIONARY PERIOD

Your employment contract will say whether your employment is subject to an initial probationary period, and if so, will say whether there are any probationary conditions and their duration.

3. JOB DUTIES

3.1 Your job title or job description is stated in your Employment Contract and/or in your Job Offer Letter, if you received a Job

Offer Letter, or as subsequently amended in writing.

3.2 You may be asked to undertake other duties that fall within your capabilities.

4. PLACE OF WORK

4.1 Your normal place of work will be set out in your Employment Contract. The Company may move your normal place of work and/or may require you to work at or transfer to other locations from time to time (also see below).

4.2 It is a condition of your employment that you to agree to transfer to wherever the Company feels necessary in the interests of the business. Such transfers are usually by mutual agreement but the Company reserves the right to make the final decision.

4.3 Where the transfer necessitates the removal of your home to a new area of work, relocation expenses may be paid at the Company's discretion.

5. WORKING HOURS

5.1 Your normal working hours are set out in your Employment Contract.

5.2 The Company reserves the right to re-arrange working hours in order to meet the needs of the business. Your working hours might be changed and you may be required to work in excess of your normal working hours.

5.3 If required, you agree to work in excess of any limit placed on working hours whether by statute or otherwise (provided in the case of a statutory limit that the requirement is lawful).

5.4 Any excess hours worked will be unpaid unless you have a specific entitlement to overtime payments, which will be set out in your Employment Contract or your Job Offer Letter, if any, or separately agreed in writing with your line manager before you work the overtime.

5.5 The Working Time Regulations specify limits on working hours and set out an employee's entitlements to rests. As an employer, we are required to monitor the hours you work to ensure you do not work longer than permitted by law. Therefore, we will monitor working hours and keep records of these hours. We may require you to keep a record of your working time and rests to assist in the monitoring process.

5.6 If you have to work during the time you usually take a meal break you may take a meal break as soon as possible thereafter making arrangements for appropriate cover when necessary

5.7 You must take a minimum rest period of 20 minutes if you have worked continuously for 6 hours. The law entitles you to a daily rest of 11 consecutive hours and a weekly rest of 24 hours. Except where we may lawfully require you to work during all or part of these rests you must take them. If as a result of our work requirements you do not get your full rest entitlements you will be entitled to an equivalent period of rest.

6. PAY

6.1 If you are paid monthly, salary payments are usually made monthly in arrears by direct credit transfer on the last of the month into an account of your choice. If the day of the month falls on a Saturday, Sunday, or Public or Bank Holiday, then the money will usually be transferred to your account on the last working day before then.

6.2 Each monthly payment covers a complete calendar month i.e. the period from the first to the last day of the month in which payment is made and your monthly pay is based on one-twelfth of your annual salary.

6.3 Salaries are usually reviewed annually for staff and the review date is normally in January. However, the Company is under no obligation to increase your salary following an annual review.

6.4 We reserve the right at any time, and in any event on termination of employment, to deduct from your pay (including holiday pay, sick pay, maternity pay and any other type of pay) any amounts that you owe. These may include season ticket loans and/ or other loans; expenses allowance; holiday taken in excess of entitlement; repayment of training expenses incurred under a training scheme; or the estimated value of any Company property damaged by you or retained by you without permission when you leave. Your final payment will reflect any adjustments, where applicable. We also reserve the right to deduct from your pay an amount equal to any allowance you receive in the course of performing public service or whilst on jury service.

6.5 Your final payment will normally be made as soon as possible following the termination of your employment.

6.6 Tax, National Insurance Contributions and any other statutory payments are deducted from your pay by the Company on a regular basis. If you need to know the address and reference number of your tax office, please ask your line manager.

6.7 We have a statutory right to make other deductions from your pay, for example, if you owe money to the Company as a result of any overpayment of remuneration or expenses or in order to comply with a court order.

7. LAY-OFFs and SHORT-TIME

7.1 The Company reserves the right to lay-off any employee without pay where no work is available for whatever reason or to place any employee on short-time working.

7.2 A lay-off is where you are not provided with work by the Company and the situation is expected to be temporary. Short-time working occurs when you are laid off for a number of contractual days each week, or for a number of hours during a working day.

7.3 During any period of lay-off you must keep in contact with the Company and must be available for work if required.

7.4 If the need for a lay-off or short-time working ever occurs you will be notified as soon as possible.

7.5 If you are laid off, you might be entitled to a statutory guarantee payment from the Company limited to a maximum of 5 days in any period of 3 months. The daily amount is subject to an upper limit which is reviewed annually by the Government. On days when a guarantee payment is not payable, it may be possible for you to claim Jobseekers Allowance through the local Jobcentre Plus office.

8. HOLIDAYS

8.1 The number of days' holiday you are entitled to in each holiday year, which runs from 1st January to 31st December is set out in your Employment Contract.

8.2 If you join the Company part way through the holiday year, your entitlement will be pro-rated within the initial holiday year.

8.3 Holiday periods should, where possible, be agreed at least 4 weeks in advance with your line manager.

8.4 You may not take more than 10 working days' holiday entitlement at one time without the prior approval of your line manager.

8.5 Payment in lieu of holiday entitlement will not normally be made except on leaving the Company.

8.6 If you resign from the Company or have been given notice of termination, you may be able to take holiday during the notice period provided that the holiday was booked and authorised before the start of the notice period. Other requests to take accrued holiday during the notice period will normally be granted but permission may be refused if business needs or other circumstances make the granting of holiday at that time impracticable.

8.7 Unused holiday entitlement may not be carried forward to the next holiday year and will be forfeited unless your line manager agrees that you may carry it forward. Where this is allowed, it will be for a maximum of one working week and must be taken by the end of March following the end of the holiday year on 31st December or it will be forfeited. However, please see the next paragraph.

8.8 If you are prevented by illness, or by maternity, paternity, adoption, parental or shared parental leave, from taking a period of holiday leave, and return to work with insufficient time to take that holiday leave within the relevant leave year, you will be allowed to take that holiday leave in the following holiday year.

8.9 Should you leave the Company, for whatever reason, your full entitlement to paid holiday will be calculated on a pro rata basis per completed week of service less any holiday entitlement taken during the holiday year. If the holiday taken exceeds your holiday entitlement, then the Company has the right to deduct payments made in excess of holiday pay entitlement from any money owing to you upon leaving.

8.10 'Pro rata' means, if you work part-time, your minimum annual holiday is calculated according to the number of days/hours you work in proportion to the Company's normal working days/hours.

8.11 Your holiday entitlement is intended to cover all holidays for whatever purpose.

8.12 The Company will make every endeavour to facilitate the observance of religious holidays within this allowance, on the assumption that cover for any religious holiday can be provided if required on a priority basis by those not affected by that particular obligation.

8.13 Salary in lieu of unused holiday entitlement is paid only on the termination of employment.

8.14 Your holiday entitlement in the year in which your employment commences or ceases (permanently or temporarily) is calculated pro rata, to the nearest half day.

8.15 A day's holiday pay will be calculated by dividing your annual salary by the number of working days, which is 260, rather than the number of calendar days.

8.16 Your holiday pay is identifiable as a separate additional sum on your payslip.

8.17 Please request holidays by completing the holiday request form available from your line manager.

8.18 You accrue paid holiday during any period of sick leave and will be allowed to take your holiday entitlement when you return to work or you will be paid holiday pay in lieu if your employment ends.

9. SICKNESS

9.1 Statutory Sick Pay (SSP) rate for the 2019/20 tax year is £94.25 per week. This is paid pro rata for fractions of the employee's working week. Income tax and NICs is deducted when appropriate. SSP is calculated by dividing the weekly rate by the number of days you would normally work in that week. For working out SSP a week runs from Sunday to Saturday.

9.2 To be eligible for SSP in the 2019/20 tax year, an employee must have average earnings of at least £118 a week.

9.3 An employer cannot pay SSP for the first 3 days of an employee's sickness; it is payable from the fourth day of absence, for a maximum of 28 weeks in any period of incapacity.

9.4 In order that SSP can be paid to you it is vital that you follow the sickness notification and certification procedures in your Employment Contract.

9.5 The sick-pay year, for calculation purposes, starts from the first period of absence in any 52-week period and all payments will include any SSP entitlement or any State Sickness Benefit.

9.6 It is a requirement of all employees who are absent due to injury or accident to notify the Company of any claim made against a third party in respect of the said injury or accident.

9.7 You must ensure the Company is notified of the reason for your absence by your normal start time on the first day of that absence or at the earliest possible opportunity thereafter.

9.8 You must keep in regular contact (daily unless otherwise agreed with your line manager) if the duration of your absence is uncertain.

9.9 If the period of absence is for 7 continuous days or less due to sickness or injury, you must report to your line manager immediately on your return to work and complete a Self-

Certification Form available from your line manager.

9.10 Failure to notify the Company on the first day of absence and to satisfactorily complete a Self-Certification form (available from your line manager) could result in payment of SSP being withheld.

9.11 In the event of that absence exceeding 7 continuous days due to sickness or injury, you must submit a Fit Note from your doctor as soon as possible. Thereafter, further Fit Notes must be submitted covering all absence until you resume work. Failure to provide Fit Notes in a timely manner could result in the non-payment of any SSP due.

9.12 Should you fail to complete the Company's Self Certification form, or provide false information, or fail to supply Fit Notes for any absence exceeding 7 continuous days, then you could have disciplinary action taken against you.

9.13 Failure to notify the Company of absence and the reason for that absence in accordance with the above rules will be regarded as unauthorised absence. Persistent or extended unauthorised absence will be considered to be misconduct and may result in disciplinary action, in accordance with the Company's disciplinary procedure.

9.14 If you attend work but then leave due to sickness before 12 noon, this will normally be recorded as one whole day's sickness absence. If you attend work but leave due to sickness after 12 noon, this will normally be recorded as a half day's sickness absence.

9.15 The Company reserves the right to obtain a medical report from your doctor subject to the Access to Medical Reports Act 1988, or to require you to undergo a medical examination by an independent medical examiner (including but not limited to an occupational health advisor), at any time prior to or during your employment. The Company will pay for any medical examination or report. Information as to your statutory rights under the Access to Medical Reports Act 1988 is available from your line manager.

9.16 If you fail to co-operate, without good reason, with a

reasonable Company requirement for you to undergo a medical examination, the Company will make an assessment based upon available information. This may lead to suspension without pay until evidence of fitness is provided or to termination of employment.

9.17 If you become unwell during the working day, you should refer to your line manager if you require permission to go home.

9.18 Under the Health and Safety Regulations the Company has a responsibility to:

9.18.1 record sickness as well as accidents;

9.18.2 advise whether it is sensible to travel home either unaccompanied or using public transport;

9.18.3 advise whether immediate medical attention is required before returning home.

9.19 Your line manager will have an informal discussion with you after each spell of absence. A more formal meeting will be held with you if your absence reaches a level which is considered to be concerning. This will usually be a total of 3 weeks of absence within the last 12 months but may be less if your line manager thinks that it is necessary. The meeting will enable your line manager to gain an understanding of the reasons for your absence and any underlying problems that you are experiencing. You will have the opportunity to discuss any problems you are having that are affecting your attendance. Any issues that come to light as a result of this discussion will be acted on as soon as reasonably possible by your line manager.

9.20 If it is believed that the sickness absence or the overall level of sickness absence is unacceptable then a formal written warning may be issued following a meeting with your line manager. The normal procedures for appeal will apply.

9.21 If you are temporarily unable to carry out a particular job activity because of health problems, but are otherwise fit to work, then it is your responsibility to make yourself available for temporary redeployment, if available, to a position which does not involve that job activity.

10. DEDUCTIONS FROM PAY

10.1 With the exception of statutory deductions e.g. PAYE, National Insurance, Court Orders, employee pension contributions, holidays taken in excess of entitlement and any deductions specified in your contract of employment, all other deductions from your pay must be authorised by you. Your written contract of employment will contain a paragraph which authorises appropriate deductions.

10.2 Examples of deductions that may be made from your pay are as follows (the list is not exhaustive):

• cash and/or stock deficiencies where an investigation has identified that the losses are as a direct result of your failure to follow Company procedures or dishonesty;

• any losses sustained in relation to Company property caused through carelessness, negligence or dishonesty;

• any damages, expenses or any other monies paid or payable by the employer to any third party for any act or omission for which you may be deemed vicariously liable;

• any amounts of remuneration, expenses or any other payments (statutory discretionary, etc) which are overpaid to you whether made by mistake or through any misrepresentation or otherwise;

• on termination of employment any holiday pay paid to you in respect of holiday granted in excess of your accrued entitlement;

• replacement of any unreturned uniforms or equipment; and

• any other sums that you may owe to the Company on termination.

11. WORKERS UNDER 18

11.1 If you are over the minimum school leaving age, but younger than 18, you must not work for more than 8 hours per day or 40 hours per week, with 2 days off per week, in accordance with current employment legislation.

11.2 You must also take a scheduled break of 30 minutes every 4 and a half hours worked, and allow a rest period of 12 hours between each working day.

11.3 Please raise any queries with your line manager.

12. PREGNANCY

All members of staff who are pregnant regardless of their length of service, have the right not to be unreasonably refused time off on full pay for ante-natal care on the advice of a registered GP, midwife or health visitor. Please ask your line manager for the Company's written Maternity Policy for more details.

13. PARENTAL LEAVE

Eligible employees can take unpaid parental leave to look after their child's welfare. Please ask your line manager for the Company's written Parental Leave Policy for more details.

14. TIME OFF FOR DEPENDANTS

14.1 You have a statutory right to unpaid time off to deal with family emergencies involving dependants. For the purpose of the right to time off, a dependant is; the employee's spouse, partner, child or parent, or someone who lives as part of the family e.g. a grandparent, or those who reasonably rely on the assistance of the employee when they are ill or injured (and do not necessarily live as part of the family), or rely on the employee to make arrangements when they are ill or injured.

14.2 It is expected that in most cases the amount of leave will be less than one day or one or 2 days at the most. However, you may be able to take longer periods where the circumstances dictate. The following examples would encompass a family emergency:

14.2.1 provide help when a dependant falls ill, is injured or assaulted;

14.2.2 assist a dependant during the birth of a child;

14.2.3 to make longer term care arrangements for a dependant who is ill or injured;

14.2.4 deal with the death of a dependant;

14.2.5 deal with unexpected disruptions/ breakdowns of care arrangements for a dependant;

14.2.6 deal with an unexpected incident involving the employee's child during school hours.

14.3 You must inform your line manager as soon as possible about your absence and how long you expect to be away from work. There may be occasions when you return to work before it is possible to contact the Company; however, on such occasions you must advise your line manager of the reason for your absence immediately upon your return to work.

15. MATERNITY LEAVE

Please ask your line manager for the Company's written Maternity Leave Policy for more details.

16. PATERNITY LEAVE

Employees whose partner has a child or who adopts a child may be entitled to paternity leave. Please ask your line manager for the Company's written Paternity Leave Policy for more details.

17. ADOPTION LEAVE

If you intend to adopt a child please ask your line manager for the Company's written Adoption Leave Policy.

18. SHARED PARENTAL LEAVE

Please ask your line manager for the Company's written Shared Parental Leave Policy for more details.

19. BEREAVEMENT LEAVE

Please ask your line manager for the Company's written Bereavement Leave Policy for more details.

19. FLEXIBLE WORKING

You may be able to request to work flexibly. Please ask your line manager for the Company's written Flexible Working Policy for more details.

20. NOTICE

20.1 The written notice required by either party is stated in your Employment Contract.

20.2 On the termination of your employment you are required to immediately return all property in your possession belonging to the Company, including all documents and any copies, security passes, computer and associated equipment including laptops, mobile phones and fax machines. You may be asked to give confirmation that you have done this.

20.3 The Company may terminate your employment summarily (i.e. with immediate effect without notice or payment in lieu of notice) if in its opinion you are guilty of gross misconduct. Examples of gross misconduct are set out in the Disciplinary Procedure.

21. RESIGNATION

21.1 You will normally be expected to work your notice period. However, on occasions, following notice either by the Company or by you, provided you continue to receive your full remuneration and benefits until your employment terminates in accordance with your contract of employment, the Company is entitled during the notice period to:

21.1.1 exclude you from the premises of the Company, or other third party at which you may be working at the relevant time on behalf of the Company; and/or

21.1.2 require you to carry out specified duties for the Company other than your normal duties; and/or

21.1.3 require you not to communicate in your capacity as a Company employee with clients or customers of the Company, other third parties designated by the Company or Company employees or officers; and/or

21.1.4 require you to refrain from attending internal and external meetings, or forums that may present a conflict or are commercially sensitive in nature.

21.2 We reserve the right to make payment in lieu of notice in relation to all or part of your notice period where you have worked some of your notice.

22. GARDEN LEAVE

22.1 At any time after notice of termination has been given (by either party) we may decide that it is appropriate to place you on "garden leave" for the remainder of your contractual notice period. The terms of this garden leave may vary depending on your role and the circumstances.

22.2 "Garden Leave" means that you are employed by the Company but you are not asked to do work.

22.2 The detail of the arrangements that could apply to you might be referred to in your contract of employment.

22.3 If you are placed on "garden leave" you will continue to be paid salary and be provided with contractual benefits during any period of garden leave in the usual way but you will not be entitled to accrue or receive any bonus or any commission during garden leave.

PART B

As stated in the Introduction, Part B is non-contractual.

24. INDUCTION

In so far as it is practical, most new employees will go through an induction with their line manager (or another member of management) on joining in order that they understand how the Company operates, their role and responsibilities including health and safety obligations.

25. PERSONAL DETAILS

25.1 If your personal details change, such as your address changes, you must tell your line manager as soon as possible.

25.2 You are required to inform the Company of anything which might impair your ability to perform your duties or your ability to render regular and efficient service. This includes matters which might adversely affect either your or the Company's reputation.

25.3 Examples of matters which would require disclosure are:

25.3.1 conviction of a criminal offence (other than a spent conviction or a minor motoring offence);

25.3.2 the laying of a criminal charge, committal for trial or an arrest; or

25.3.3 any disqualification by law from doing your job.

26. PERSONAL DATA

26.1 As your employer we will need to retain data about you on both paper and electronic files whilst you are employed and for a period of seven years following your employment.

26.2 This data is for internal use and will be processed in line with the principles of the General Data Protection Regulation (GDPR). As far as is reasonable, information processed will be restricted to current, relevant information access which will be restricted to individuals who have a genuine need to process or deal with it.

26.3 Access by individuals external to the Company is only provided where your consent is given or where there is a statutory or legal need to provide it or where you are clearly aware of this use.

26.4 Employees are allowed access to personal data held about them. We reserve the right to charge an administrative fee for providing personal data.

27. BONUSES

27.1 If you are eligible for a performance bonus this will be set out in your Employment Contract or in a Job Offer letter or in a separate document. In any event, the decision as to whether or not to award a bonus, the amount of any award, and the timing and form of the award are at the discretion of the Company. Factors which may be taken into account by the Company in deciding whether or not to award a bonus are also at the discretion of the Company.

27.2 No bonus, even if awarded, will be paid to you if at the date payment of the bonus would normally have been made you are not employed by the Company or if you are under notice to leave the Company whether such notice was given or received by you.

27.3 All bonus payments are subject to tax as part of your earnings and may not qualify as pensionable earnings.

28. EXPENSES

28.1 You will normally be entitled to be reimbursed for all reasonable business expenses (including travel and accommodation), providing you obtain authorisation from your line manager before incurring the expenditure, unless this is not possible or not reasonably practical.

28.2 You must show receipts for the expenses you are reclaiming, such as hotel bills.

28.3 Parking charges may be reclaimed, if incurred on the Company's business, on the presentation of a receipt or an expired parking ticket.

28.4 Parking fines will not be paid under any circumstances.

28.5 If driving your vehicle on Company business, or a Company vehicle, it is your duty to ensure that any payments due under the London congestion charging scheme, or other city charging schemes, are paid by the due time so as not to avoid any surcharge or penalty for late payment.

28.6 Falsification of expense claims is likely to be considered as gross misconduct and subject to disciplinary action leading to a possible summary dismissal.

29. LOANS

29.1 The Company may, at its discretion, give you an interest free loan, for example, to enable you to purchase an annual season ticket for travel to and from work. Applications for loans should be made to your line manager.

29.2 Repayment of the loan will be made over an agreed period by equal monthly deductions from your salary.

29.3 If you leave our employment before the loan is repaid the amount outstanding will be deducted from your final salary payment.

30. TRAINING

30.1 The Company recognises that it is essential to train and develop employees at all levels to enable the business to meet its objectives, enable employees to achieve their career aspirations and to reach their full potential.

30.2 Some of the training will be compulsory for all appropriate employees, for example, training related to health and safety issues. However, some training will be optional and offered at the Company's discretion.

30.3 Employees wishing to be supported on professional or technical qualification may seek Company assistance and, if granted, will be subject to an individual Training Agreement. In addition, in such cases should you leave within 12 months of completing the training, the following deductions may be made from your final pay.

30.3.1   Before completion 100% of cost;

30.3.2   Up to 3 Months 75% of cost;

30.3.3   3 - 6 Months 50% of cost;

30.3.4   6 - 12 Months 25% of cost.

31. APPRAISALS

31.1 An appraisal meeting with your line manager is usually held at least once a year. These meetings are designed to give you and your line manager the opportunity to review your performance, to agree objectives and to identify personal development plans. It is also an important opportunity for you to raise any issues and concerns you might have about your work with your line manager.

31.2 Employees are entitled to see all of their appraisal reports and have the opportunity to sign the completed form and to express their views on the appraisal they have received; in particular whether they feel it is a fair assessment of their work over the reporting period.

31.3 Employees may appeal against their assessment if they think it was unfair to a different manager than the appraiser by using the Grievance Procedure. The Grievance Procedure is referred to in your Employment Contract and also set out below.

32. IMPROVEMENT

If your performance is not up to a standard reasonably required by the Company your line manager will discuss the required improvements with you and agree the improvements required with a timescale for improvement. If you think your line manager in being unreasonable in any way you can raise a formal grievance under the Company's Grievance Procedure which is referred to in your Employment Contract and also set out below.

33. TIMEKEEPING

You should attend work on the days and times set out in your Employment Contract and, in addition, agree to be available for work on any day when the Company requires you to work. You are expected to be at work by your scheduled start time. Persistent lateness will not be tolerated and may lead to disciplinary action.

34. SIGNING IN AND OUT

34.1 If you are required to sign in or out you must ensure that you sign in on arrival and sign-out on departure from the premises.

34.2 In the event of failing to sign in or out when required, you must report to your line manager and advise of the exact time of arrival or departure, and the reason for failing to sign in or out. It will be at the Company's discretion to make the appropriate entry on the record sheet. You must never complete entries on the sheet for yourself without express authority from a member of senior management.

34.3 You must never sign for another employee, or request or allow another employee to sign in or out on your behalf.

34.4 If you sign in or out for another employee, or allow another employee to sign for you, you will be liable to disciplinary being taken against you.

34.5 For the avoidance of doubt, a reference to 'signing in and out' includes a reference to 'clocking in and out'.

34.6 Please contact your line manager if you require more information.

35. DRESS CODE

We expect you to present a clean and professional appearance when representing the Company, whether that is in or outside of any of the Company's premises or on Company business. If in doubt please ask your line manager what is considered as appropriate business clothing and appearance for your role.

36. OTHER EMPLOYMENT

36.1 You are not permitted to work in any capacity for a business that carries out work of a similar type to the Company's.

36.2 If you choose to take up additional employment outside your normal working hours, this might be accepted by the Company unless such additional employment is felt to have an adverse affect on:

36.2.1 the performance of your normal duties with the Company; and/or

36.2.2 your health and safety.

36.3 The Company has a legal obligation to monitor the total number of hours its employees work each week, and it is your responsibility to notify the Company in writing of other employment including the number of hours you work for any other employer. Failure to notify the Company will be considered a disciplinary matter.

36.4 'Other employment' includes casual or part-time work in your spare time (whether paid or not) and employment includes directorships, trusteeships, school governorships, local authority councillorships, or provision of services as a consultant or agent.

37. ABSENCES FROM WORK

37.1 If you wish to leave work during working hours, you must obtain permission from your line manager.

37.2 When personal circumstances prevent you from attending work, you must notify your line manager by your normal start time or at the earliest possible opportunity to discuss the reasons for the absence. Your line manager may exercise discretion in authorising a specific period of absence with or without pay, or agree to annual holiday being taken at short notice to cover the absence required. Where the circumstances are of a confidential nature they will be kept confidential.

37.3 Normally paid leave for purposes other than holidays, compassionate leave, sickness or jury service is not allowed. However, it is recognised that there are occasionally unplanned 'emergencies' outside of the control of a member of staff which necessitate an absence from work; for example, a burst pipe or other hazard posing an imminent threat to your home, where you are the victim of a burglary or other crime, or where severe weather conditions make your journey to work impossible in spite of your best efforts to get in. These examples differ from 'planned' incidents, for example, publicised transport strikes and engineering works when you would be expected to make every effort to plan ahead so that you are able to attend the office even if this is at some inconvenience to you.

37.4 In the case of an 'unplanned' emergency each case will be reviewed on an individual basis and you should contact your line manager as soon as possible to discuss the situation. This may result in your having to use part of your leave allowance or make up the time lost if this is a practical option. You must follow the same notification procedure as with sickness absence.

37.5 Unpaid leave will normally only be granted in exceptional circumstances and when all paid holiday entitlement is exhausted. Requests for unpaid leave should be directed to your line manager.

37.6 Regardless of whether the absence is authorised, where an employee is absent from work on more than three occasions within a six month period, we reserve the right to invite the employee to an investigatory meeting.

38. MEDICAL APPOINTMENTS

We recognise that everyone may need to attend certain appointments from time to time. Any appointments should be made outside working hours wherever possible with your line manager's permission, or at a time to ensure minimum disruption of your work. You must provide advance notice of any such appointments to your line manager, unless this is not possible, and you may be required to provide documentary evidence of the appointment.

39. MEDICAL EXAMINATIONS

39.1 The Company reserves the right, in the event of an employee's absence(s), either to require an employee to undergo a medical examination by a doctor appointed by the Company or to request the employee's permission to obtain a medical report from the employee's doctor, subject to an employee's legal right under the Access to Medical Reports Act 1988.

39.2 If the employee fails to attend an appointment or does not allow the Company to access relevant medical records, we reserve the right to make a decision based upon the information that we can reasonably obtain.

39.3 If an employee does not attend an arranged medical appointment, without a good reason, the employee will be liable for any costs incurred by the Company as a result of the non-attendance. The employee might also be subject to disciplinary action if there was no good reason for the non-attendance.

40. JURY SERVICE

If you are called for Jury Service you must notify your line manager immediately. You will be asked to provide evidence of attendance at court. You are required to claim from the Court Authorities the full amount of your loss of earnings. As your employer we do not have to pay you whilst you are on jury service. But you can claim for travel and food expenses and for loss of earnings from the Court. You need to ask your line manager to fill out a Certificate of Loss of Earnings to claim for loss of earnings from the Court Authorities. There are limits on the amount that you can claim. The Company is not bound to make up any balance to your basic wages or salary but may do so at its discretion. You should attend work on any days or half days when you are not required by the Court.

41. ATTENDING COURT

If you are subpoenaed or otherwise compelled by a Court to attend the same points apply as for jury service. However, if your attendance in Court as a witness is on an voluntary basis, you would normally be required to take any day when you are needed in Court as part of your holiday entitlement or as unpaid leave.

42. PUBLIC DUTIES

An employee who is a Justice of the Peace or a member of a Local Authority, Health or Education Body, a statutory Tribunal, a Police Authority, a Board of Prison Visitors or the Environment Agency or a similar Body is allowed to take a reasonable amount of time off unpaid for the purposes of attending meetings or undertaking their duties as a member of such a Body.

43. FORCES RESERVIST

If you are a Voluntary Reservist and are required to take part in annual training camps, you will be allowed to take 2 weeks per annum for such purpose, so long as you have normally provided at least 8 weeks notice to your line manager of your intention to take leave, along with documentary evidence. It is expected that one week of this will be taken as part of your annual holiday entitlement and the other week will be granted as unpaid leave. For the week of unpaid leave you will be entitled to claim the appropriate payment from the Armed Forces. If you are mobilised we do not have to pay you any salary or associated benefits for the duration of your operational duty. When you return from mobilisation we will reinstate you in the same role and on equally favourable terms and conditions as before, or as near as practicable.

44. RELIGIOUS HOLIDAYS

We will not discriminate against employees on the grounds of religious beliefs. Reasonable unpaid leave (or paid if you choose to take it as holiday) will be granted for a religious holiday or festival or to observe your religious beliefs. You should follow the same process for booking any such time off with your line manager as you would for normal holidays.

45. COMPASSIONATE LEAVE

Compassionate Leave for the loss of a close relative or friend may be authorised only at the discretion of your line manager. It is at the Company's discretion as to the amount of leave granted and whether it will be paid, part-paid or unpaid.

46. BAD WEATHER

46.1 In the event of extreme adverse weather conditions, e.g. heavy snow, flooding, storms etc., you are expected to make every attempt to arrive at work at your normal starting time as long as it is safe to do so.

46.2 If you decide that the weather conditions will prevent you from travelling to work you must normally opt to either: take the day(s) as holiday, or; take the day(s) as authorised unpaid leave of absence, or; if appropriate, work from home. You must telephone your line manager by your normal start time to discuss the situation and the option you wish to take. If your line manager is not available, you must ensure that another suitable member of staff is notified of your absence.

46.3 In the event you decide to travel to work and then subsequently find that the weather conditions prevent you from completing your journey, you must telephone your line manager within 2 hours of your normal starting time, or as soon as possible if it is safe and legal to do so, and inform him or her of the exact circumstances. In this case, the Company at its discretion, in light of the circumstances, will decide whether or not you will qualify for full pay.

46.4 In any event, your absence or lateness from work due to extreme adverse weather conditions will not be subject to the Company's disciplinary procedure provided you notify the Company in accordance with the above policy.

47. SAFETY AT WORK

47.1 You must comply with all the Company's procedures and instructions regarding health and safety procedures. Failure to obey may be misconduct or gross misconduct depending on how serious the failure is deemed to be.

47.1 Health and safety procedures may change from time to time and you must ensure that you read and understand any notices about changes. If in doubt, please ask your line manager.

47.2 You are reminded that you are responsible for ensuring that you act in a safe and sensible manner whilst at work and failure to do so will lead to disciplinary action by the Company and possibly criminal proceedings under Health and Safety legislation.

47.3 You must have regard to your own health and safety. For example, if you are required, in the course of your work, to move heavy objects, you should familiarise yourself with the manual handling procedures. If in doubt, do not hesitate to contact your line manager for advice, instructions or assistance before undertaking any hazardous or potentially hazardous tasks.

47.4 If you habitually use display screen equipment as a significant part of your work, you will be provided with a free eye and eyesight test upon request. If the test results in you needing to wear glasses specifically for VDU work, the Company will contribute towards the cost of a basic pair of glasses or replacement lenses. Details of your entitlement to an eye-test are available from your line manager.

47.5 You must not work if you have taken medication or any other substance which could adversely affect your ability to operate equipment or in any other way inhibit your ability to work safely.

47.6 You must read and comply with all notices, instructions, hazard and warning signs provided from time to time for your information.

47.7 Please bring any problems you may have with your work environment or work station to the attention of your line manager.

47.8 We have a responsibility under the Health & Safety legislation to ensure that people who are not employees of the Company are not exposed to risks to their health and safety while working for the Company as a contractor or visiting our premises. You are expected to do everything possible to assist the Company in complying with this responsibility.

47.9 To sum up, all employees have a legal responsibility under the Health and Safety at Work legislation to pay attention and adhere to the contents of any statutory warning, informatory notices, training and instruction provided and to carry out regular risk assessments of their workplace and work procedures and point out any potential areas of risk.

48. PROTECTIVE CLOTHING AND EQUIPMENT

When instructed to do so you must wear the protective clothing and equipment provided. Failure to comply with such an instruction may be regarded as an act of misconduct and dealt with through the Company's disciplinary procedure.

49. ACCIDENTS AT WORK

49.1 If you see a situation in which a potential accident could occur or where an injury could be sustained by anyone in your workplace you should report it immediately to your line manager.

49.2 All accidents, injuries, and cases of ill–health caused by, or affecting, your work must be reported to your line manager without delay. If you are injured, no matter how slight your injury may appear, you must always report it to your line manager and ensure that you are seen by a first–aider and that the details of your accident or injury are entered in the Accident Book. Your line manager will tell you where the Accident Book is kept if you do not know. All dangerous occurrences and 'near miss' incidents should also be reported in the same way.

49.3 As an employer, the Company has legal obligations under the Health and Safety legislation to ensure the health of our employees at work. We are committed to creating a working environment that minimises the risk to your health. This means ensuring that the demands of your job are reasonable and you are adequately trained and supported to undertake your role. It means doing our best to give you as much control as possible over how your work is planned and carried out and dealing promptly with issues such as unacceptable behaviour by colleagues.

49.4 Ultimately, you have primary responsibility for your own health and wellbeing. It is up to you to take reasonable care of yourself and to let us know about any aspect of work or your working environment which may be affecting your health.

49.5 If you feel that you need additional support or guidance to maintain your wellbeing at work, you should to talk to your line manager, or another senior member of management. This will allow you to raise concerns about your volume of work, some training that you may need or to discuss any personality issues with colleagues.

49.6 Any discussion regarding your health will be treated in the strictest confidence and information will only be released with your permission. It is clearly in everyone's interest that you raise issues early so that they can be dealt with.

49.7 Every employee involved in an accident at work, whether a road traffic accident or involving Company equipment or an accident occurring on any of the Company's premises, may be required to undertake a test to determine whether alcohol and / or non-medically prescribed drugs are present. If an employee tests positive for alcohol and / or non-medically prescribed drugs then the employee is likely to be be suspended with pay for the rest of the working day, subject to further investigation and disciplinary action up to and including dismissal.

50. FIRST AID

It is your responsibility to know the location of first aid boxes and the name of anyone trained in first aid. Ask your line manager if you do not have this information.

51. FIRE DRILL

51.1 In the case of fire, you must evacuate the building in

accordance with the fire instructions. It is your responsibility to be aware of these instructions and where the nearest fire exit and fire appliances are located.

51.2 Any concerns you may have about fire hazards should also be addressed to your line manager so that appropriate measures can be taken to eliminate the problem.

51.3 Attempts to extinguish the fire should only be made if it is safe to do so.

51.4 Assemble at the designated fire assembly point.

51.5 Do not run, use lifts or stop to collect personal belongings.

51.6 Do not re-enter the building until instructed that it is safe to do so.

52. BOMB ALERTS

52.1 It is not possible to be definite about what to do in the event of a bomb warning but the following general rules should be observed:

52.1.1 do exactly what you are told by the emergency services if they are present;

52.1.2 do whatever is necessary and sensible to reduce the risk of injury, i.e. if there is a known bomb threat and you have not been told to evacuate the building, retire to the safest area within your building. This will normally be away from the risk of broken/flying glass;

52.1.3 if you are in the building out of normal working hours and an incident takes place, either directly affecting the building or in the close vicinity, the most senior person present must take responsibility for notifying the Company management of the situation;

52.1.4 If you are in the vicinity of an incident away from the office and your whereabouts or safety may be uncertain, please contact the Company as soon as possible;

52.1.5 the safety of staff and visitors is always paramount. Never jeopardise personal safety in the interest of safeguarding property or information;

52.1.6 if the building is seriously damaged as a result of a major incident which occurs outside normal office hours or at a time when you are not present in the building, you should not return to the building until you have received instructions from the Company.

53. NO SMOKING POLICY

53.1 Smoking is prohibited on and in all Company premises or in any Company vehicles. Failure to comply with this prohibition is likely to lead to disciplinary action up to and including dismissal.

53.2 This policy applies to all employees, contractors, consultants and visitors to our premises.

53.3 If a visitor does not comply with the no-smoking policy they should firstly be asked to extinguish the smoking material. If they continue to smoke they should be asked to leave.

54. ENVIRONMENTAL RESPONSIBILITY

54.1 We are committed to improving our overall impact on the environment through responsible practices. All employees are responsible for ensuring that these values are maintained at all times. We are particularly concerned about reducing our carbon footprint by minimising greenhouse gas emissions.

54.2 All employees are expected to ensure that energy usage including gas, electricity, oil, water, transport and waste materials are managed to minimise our environmental impact.

55. DRUGS AND ALCOHOL

55.1 The Company forbids the consumption of alcohol or the use or distribution of substances for non-medically prescribed purposes, in any of its premises whilst you are at work for the Company or whilst driving a Company vehicle or another vehicle on Company business. If we believe you are under the influence of alcohol or non-medically prescribed drugs, and not fit to work, we reserve the right to suspend you, pending further investigation. Similarly, if you are found with, or having been using, any such substances during working hours, you may be suspended and subject to disciplinary action, up to and including dismissal for gross misconduct.

55.2 Furthermore, where reasonable suspicion exists that an employee may be under the influence of illegal/non-prescribed drugs or excessive amounts of alcohol, the Company also reserves the right to request that such employee undertakes a test to determine the levels of alcohol and/ or non-medically prescribed drugs present. Failure to agree to undertake a test will be viewed as a breach of contract and the appropriate disciplinary action will be invoked, up to and including dismissal. If the test is positive and the individual is found to be under the influence of drugs or is over the legal alcohol limit to drive a vehicle, the Company may take any action it deems fit, including disciplinary action up to and including dismissal for gross misconduct. Failure to attend or complete a course of counselling, where deemed appropriate, may also be viewed as an act of gross misconduct.

55.3 Always advise your line manager if you are taking prescribed medication as this may affect your health and safety and fitness to work. In certain circumstances we may seek permission to obtain a medical report under the Access to Medical Records Act 1988, or to require you to undergo a medical examination by an independent medical examiner. The Company will pay for any medical examination or report.

56. CONFIDENTIALITY

56.1 You acknowledge that in the course of your employment you may have access to and be entrusted with confidential information.

56.2 You shall not during your employment or afterwards, use or exploit or disclose directly or indirectly to any other person by any means any confidential information except that which you shall be permitted to do so:

56.2.1 when necessary in the proper performance of the duties of your employment;

56.2.2 with the written permission of the Company; or

56.2.3 where this is required by law.

56.3 You shall not, during your employment or at any time thereafter make any copy, record, or memorandum (whether or not recorded in writing or on computer disk or tape, data stick or other transportable media) of any confidential information without permission, and any such copy record or memorandum made by you during your employment shall be and remains the property of the Company and accordingly shall be returned by you to the Company on termination of your employment.

56.4 You will not use for your own purposes, or profit or for any purposes other than those of the Company, any confidential information which you may acquire in relation to the Company's and/or its customers.

56.5 The rules concerning disclosure of confidential information apply both during and after your employment with the Company.

56.6 Unauthorised access to confidential information, whether computerised or manual, may lead to disciplinary action. In the case of computerised information 'hacking' will be considered a dismissible offence.

56.7 'Confidential information' means:

56.7.1 all information which relates to the business, finances, transactions, dealings, affairs, products, services, processes, equipment, information with respect to the identity or businesses of the customers and suppliers of the Company and details of contracts, quotations, time scales, prices, discounts or any other aspect of a contract or potential contract, or activities of the Company which is designated by the Company as confidential; and

56.7.2 all information relating to such matters which comes to your knowledge in the course of your employment and which, by reason of its character and/or the manner of its coming to your knowledge, is evidently confidential; and

56.7.3 provided that information shall not be, or shall cease to be, confidential information if and to the extent that it comes to be in the public domain otherwise than as a result of the unauthorised act or default by you.

56.8 Breach of confidentiality will normally result in disciplinary action being taken and may ultimately result in the termination of your employment.

57. EQUAL OPPORTUNITIES

57.1 The Company is committed to providing a working environment and conditions where all employees are treated equally and on the basis of their merits, abilities and potential, regardless of gender, colour, and ethnic or national origin, disability, social-economic background, religious or political beliefs, family circumstances (including pregnancy, maternity), age, gender re-assignment, marital circumstances, sexual orientation or other irrelevant distinction.

57.2 Discrimination, in any form, is unacceptable to the Company and will be considered a disciplinary offence, which, dependant upon the severity, may be considered gross misconduct warranting summary dismissal.

57.3 All employees have a personal responsibility to adhere to this policy by treating all colleagues and anyone else connected with, or visiting the Company, fairly and impartially.

58. BULLYING and HARASSMENT

58.1 The Company will take all reasonable steps to ensure that the workplace should be free from bullying, intimidation, harassment, victimisation and discrimination.

58.2 'Bullying and harassment' is considered by the Company to be any physical, verbal or non-verbal behaviour that is unwanted and/or offensive and which creates an intimidating or humiliating working environment that undermines employee's dignity in or relating to the workplace.

58.3 Anyone found to have bullied or harassed will be subject to disciplinary action for gross misconduct.

58.4 All employees have a responsibility to ensure that their own behaviour does not amount to bullying or harassment.

58.5 Employees should report all incidents of bullying or harassment to their line manager or to a senior member of management.

58.6 You are reminded that any complaint you have can be addressed using the Company's written Grievance Procedure. All such complaints will be dealt with seriously, sensitively and in the strictest confidence.

59. COMPANY PROPERTY

59.1 You are not allowed to take Company property off the Company's premises unless you have permission from your line manager. The Company reserves the right to have access to and/or to retrieve any items of its property on demand.

59.2 Employees are expected to maintain a reasonable level of care and security of Company property in their possession at all times.

59.3 Failure to take appropriate care of Company property and premises may result in a personal liability to replace the item(s) and, in some instances, disciplinary action.

59.4 When your employment with the Company ends you are required to return, in a good condition, any Company property such as PC equipment, iPhones, uniforms, documents, manuals, utensils, tools, books etc.

59.5 The Company reserves the right to make an appropriate deduction from any wages or other payments owed by the Company to you in respect of any Company property that you do not return or you do not return in a satisfactory condition.

60. EMPLOYEE'S PROPERTY

60.1 Any personal property brought onto the Company's premises or vehicles are the responsibility of the individual and the Company accepts no liability for any loss or damage. Employees must safeguard any valuables by keeping them on their person or by locking them away.

60.2 An employee's property or personal belongings will not be covered by the Company's Insurances.

60.3 If an employee is entitled to park in the Company's car park this is at the employee's risk and the Company will not accept liability for the theft of the car or its contents or damage thereto.

61. RIGHT TO SEARCH

61.1 The Company reserves the right to search you and any of your property held on Company premises at any time if there are reasonable grounds to believe that the search will result in the finding of evidence of criminal activity or an activity detrimental to the interests of the Company.

61.2 Any search will be conducted by a senior member of management with your consent in the presence of an agreed witness.

61.3 Where a personal search is necessary, this will be carried out by a person of the same sex as the person being searched.

61.4 Searches will be carried out courteously, sensitively and discreetly. An individual has the right to be searched in a private room.

61.5 You may refuse to permit the personal search and there is no disciplinary sanction for this. However, as the grounds which give rise to the request to search you may amount to misconduct, we may invoke the disciplinary procedure in relation to those grounds.

61.6 We may at anytime invite the police to search Company premises and/or people present on Company premises who are suspected of criminal or other illegal activity.

62. STOCK and CASH

62.1 The Company reserves the right to check stock and cash at any time without notice.

62.2 If any deficiency in cash and/or stock is found the Company reserves the right to require the person or persons whom it has reasonable cause to believe is or are responsible for making good the deficiency.

62.3 If, after an appropriate investigation, the Company has reasonable cause to believe that the deficiency is due to serious negligence or deliberate action on the part of any employee, disciplinary action will be taken against that employee.

63. EXPENDITURE

You have no authority to commit the company to any expenditure unless you have been given prior written authority.

64. SECURITY OF PREMISES

Where premises become insecure due to break-ins etc., key-holders for the premises are required to remain at the premises until the premises can be secured. If necessary the key-holders should organise a rota for covering the premises.

65. CCTV MONITORING

65.1 If the Company's premises are protected by closed circuit television (CCTV) cameras these will be stationed at various points in the Company's premises, including entrances and exits, secure areas of the building and certain storage and/or emergency areas. The cameras may or may not be visible for reasons of security.

65.2 Footage from the cameras will be monitored regularly around the clock to ensure that we are alerted to any suspicious or dangerous activity, including possible breaches of security or the commission of an offence.

65.3 The purpose of CCTV cameras is to prevent, detect and investigate crime and to apprehend and prosecute offenders. It is also used for the health and safety of our staff and visitors and to monitor security on Company premises.

65.4 The relevant provisions of current data protection legislation apply to any CCTV data held about you. You can obtain information about this data protection legislation from your line manager.

66. ID PASSES

66.1 If you are issued with a security ID pass, you must wear and display your pass at all times when inside Company premises and present it to any security staff on request. Your security pass must not be loaned or given to others (whether Company staff or not). If you lose your pass you must report the matter immediately to your line manager. Security passes are the property of the Company and must be returned at the end of your employment or engagement.

66.2 In the interests of security and safety, you should not bring friends or relatives or other of your visitors into staff-only areas without prior approval from your line manager.

67. VISITORS

Visitors may be provided with a visitor's badge for identification purposes, in which case, they will be required to wear and display their badges at all times. They will not be permitted in staff-only areas unless accompanied at all times by a member of staff. If you are the visitor's host, you are responsible for ensuring that security and safety are maintained.

68. DATA PROTECTION

68.1 You must at all times act in accordance with any policy or instruction introduced by the Company to ensure compliance with current data protection legislation. Ask your line manager for more information if you need it.

68.2 The aim of the Company is to strike a balance between the right of an employee to respect for his or her private life and the needs of the business. In the interests of the business, you must agree to the following:

68.2.1 the Company processing any personal data relating to you;

68.2.2 the Company processing any sensitive personal data relating to you including, without being restricted to, bank account details, any self-certification forms or medical certificates supplied to the Company to explain your absence by reason of sickness or injury, any records of sickness absence, any medical reports or health assessments, any details of your trade union membership, if any, or any information relating to any criminal convictions or any criminal charges secured or brought against you; and

68.2.3 the Company collecting and disclosing your personal data (including sensitive personal data) from time to time where such processing is necessary or reasonably required by the Company for the performance of your contact of employment, the conduct of the Company's business or the proper administration and management of the employment relationship (both during and after your employment) or where such processing is required by law.

68.3 For its part the Company will take steps to ensure that it complies with its legal obligations in relation to the processing of your personal data and in particular will put procedures in place to ensure that all your personal data held by the Company is accurate and up to date and is not kept for longer than necessary. Measures will also be taken to safeguard against unauthorised or unlawful processing and accidental loss or destruction or damage to the data.

68.4 If the nature of your job means that you have access to data regarding the Company and/or anyone associated with the Company, including but not limited to other employees and customers, you must not disclose the data to unauthorised persons or use it for purposes other than the legitimate purpose(s) for which it was collected.

68.5 Any unauthorised disclosure or negligence in relation to data protection may result in disciplinary action which could result in dismissal.

68.6 Persons can incur criminal liability if they knowingly or recklessly obtain and/or disclose personal information without appropriate authority.

69. COMPUTERS and INTERNET

69.1 There are laws regulating computers and data protection with which the Company must comply. In particular, it is illegal to make copies of software. Software issued to you by the Company is licensed to the Company and is protected by copyright law. You must not make or distribute software that has been copied. It is therefore important that all employees minimise exposure to risk through careless practices with regard to the use of data or inappropriate, or illegal, use of software.

69.2 Employees supplied with computer equipment are responsible for that equipment, and the security of software and data stored either on their own system or other systems which they can access remotely.

69.3 You are not permitted to use the Company computer facilities for personal use without the permission of the Company and computers should only be used by you to perform your job. You are only authorised to use systems and have access to information which is relevant to your job. You should neither seek information or use systems outside of this criteria.

69.4 Any misuse of the Company's computers and internet access will be considered a disciplinary matter. Accessing pornographic or gambling sites, for example, will be considered as gross misconduct likely to result in a summary dismissal.

69.5 You should at all times keep your personal password confidential. When changing your password you should adopt a password which does not use personal data. You should change your password regularly and you must never share or divulge your personal password to any unauthorised person.

69.6 You must immediately inform your line manager if you become aware of any copyright infringements of software or associated materials within the Company or of any other misuse of the Company's computer systems. You are referred to the paragraph giving information on 'whistleblowing'.

69.7 Communications via the internet and by the Company's internal electronic email system are intrinsically insecure and may be intercepted and you should not transmit confidential information via this means. Email should be treated with the same caution as the ordinary written communication; e-mail messages should not be treated as conversations, they are more permanent. You should print off and file important business related e-mails in the same way as you would letters and memos.

69.8 You must not knowingly access, view, download or forward any illegal, inappropriate or in any way offensive material (e.g. pornography, discriminatory jokes, etc) under any circumstances. You may cause offence when none is intended. You should check the content of email messages before you sent them to ensure that they may not be construed by recipients as harassment or abuse of any kind. You should also ensure that your message will not be sent dishonestly or in bad faith.

69.9 The Company reserves the right to monitor, and wherever necessary, review the history of communications made via any of its information technology and telecommunications systems. This includes access to the internet via the Company's systems.

69.10 The purpose of this monitoring is to ensure that the Company's systems are used primarily to further the business of the Company, that they are not used for inappropriate and/or unlawful purposes and that system capacity is sufficient for the needs of the business.

69.11 The content of communications will be monitored only where absolutely necessary. However you should be aware that such monitoring may take place and that the content of your communications using the Company's systems cannot therefore be regarded as completely confidential.

69.12 Wherever possible monitoring will be:

69.12.1 done automatically;

69.12.2 limited to the assessment of traffic;

69.12.3 take the form of spot checks or audits rather than be carried out continuously; and

69.12.4 be targeted at areas of highest risk or where a particular problem is indicated.

70. SOCIAL MEDIA

Individual employees, as well as our Company, can be held personally liable for comments made via social media on the internet, such as Facebook or Twitter. Any employee using social media or other online communication channels must ensure that they do nothing which could cause a third party to take legal action, such as a claim for defamation, against the Company or any person or business connected with the Company.

71 COMPANY MOBILE TELEPHONES

71.1 If you are provided with a mobile telephone, this is to be used for business calls only. You must not use a mobile phone belonging to the Company for your personal use without the permission of the Company.

71.2 If the mobile telephone is used for private telephone calls, even with permission, the Company may require you to reimburse the cost of these calls.

71.3 You should take care of the mobile telephone and ensure it is secure at all times. In the event that the telephone is stolen you should notify your line manager immediately to report the theft so that steps can be taken to disconnect the telephone, and if possible, wipe data on it.

71.4 The mobile telephone should be immediately returned to the Company if you are requested to do so by your line manager or on the termination of your employment.

71.5 The use of handheld mobile phones whilst driving is illegal and will be considered a disciplinary matter.

72. PERSONAL TELEPHONE CALLS

72.1 You may only make private telephone calls using your own mobile phone during breaks unless it is an emergency.

72.2 The use of Company telephones for personal reasons requires the permission of your line manager and you may be asked to reimburse the cost of the call.

72.3 In an emergency, calls will be accepted by the Company and the message(s) passed to you as appropriate.

73. OWN MOTOR VEHICLES ON COMPANY BUSINESS

73.1 In general, private cars should be used only for journeys where public transport is inappropriate.

73.2 If you need to use your own car on Company business, you should only do so with the prior approval of your line manager, and you should ensure that the vehicle is insured for business use, taxed and, where applicable, has an MOT certificate and that you hold a valid driving licence.

73.3 You may not claim the cost of travel between home and your normal place of work.

73.4 Taxis should be used appropriately and only when public transport is unavailable or impractical. You should ask the taxi driver for a receipt and then reclaim your expenses by the usual method.

73.5 Breaking the law when driving on Company business, for example, using a mobile phone in your hand whilst driving, will be considered a disciplinary matter even if you are driving your own car.

73.6 Any travelling expenses incurred in undertaking Company duties in your own vehicle will be reimbursed by the Company, at Inland Revenue approved rates, according to the number of miles travelled, and you must keep an accurate record of such mileage, and if required, justify the route taken.

74. COMPANY MOTOR VEHICLES

74.1 If you are supplied with a Company car the terms will be detailed in a letter to you.

74.2 Due to insurance reasons, only those in the employ of the Company are allowed as passengers in the Company's vans or commercial vehicles whether on public or private roads.

74.3 Whilst a vehicle is allocated to you, it must remain of a clean and tidy appearance on the inside and outside.

74.4 As soon as a vehicle defect is discovered on the vehicle, it must be reported to your line manager or a senior member of management immediately for a decision to be taken as to whether the vehicle is roadworthy.

74.5 It is an offence to drive or send a vehicle on the road with a defect which renders a vehicle as 'unroadworthy' even if unknowingly. As the driver of the vehicle it is your legal duty to ensure that the vehicle you drive is roadworthy. You, as well as the Company, face prosecution by the police if you are driving a vehicle which is unroadworthy.

74.6 In the event that you are allocated a vehicle that you have not used before, please ask your line manager or a senior member of management if there are any specific requirements for the vehicle.

74.7 Never drive a vehicle that you are not confident about using. The Company is conscious of its responsibility both to its employees and other road users.

75. COMMERCIAL VEHICLES

On joining the Company, drivers of commercial vehicles may be required to attend driver training as part of their induction, and on an ongoing basis for refresher training or development. Failure to attend such training or development could result in disciplinary action being taken which could result in dismissal.

76. 'WHISTLEBLOWING'

76.1 If you have concerns about malpractice in the Company it can be difficult to know what to do or who to tell.

'Whistleblowing' (known legally as 'making a protected disclosure') legislation provides a way of informing those in authority inside and outside the Company of your concerns.

76.2 Malpractice might cover criminal activity, breach of legal regulations, endangering somebody's health or safety, environmental damage, abuse of office or position or any attempt by any person to conceal any such matters.

76.3 If you have a concern or reasonable suspicion about malpractice, you should raise this with your line manager or a senior member of the Company. They will discuss your concern with you and, following that discussion, decide how to proceed.

76.4 If you do not wish to contact a member of the Company initially, or if you wish to talk through your concerns with another party, you might want to contact Public Concern at Work, an independent charity providing confidential advice on whistleblowing. Their website is at 'www.pcaw.org.uk' (the web address or name might have changed when you need to make contact but a 'google' search should find their new website).

76.5 Where requested, reasonable efforts will be made to ensure that your identity is not revealed to those who might be involved in suspected malpractice. Your identity will be revealed only where this is reasonably necessary to investigate or deal with suspected malpractice and, if this happens, all reasonable steps will be taken to ensure that you are not disadvantaged as a result.

76.6 You will be kept informed of any investigation and any action taken in relation to your concern. You will not be penalised for raising a concern.

77. BRIBERY

77.1 Anyone providing services for or on behalf of the Company, including but not limited to employees, temporary workers, contractors and sub-contractors of the Company are bound by the Bribery Act 2010 which makes bribery a criminal offence.

77.2 The Bribery Act created four offences of bribery: 1) Giving bribes; 2) Receiving bribes; 3) Bribing a foreign public official; and 4) Corporate offence of failing to prevent bribery. You must inform your line manager or a senior member of management if you have reason to believe that bribery is taking place.

78. CONFLICT OF INTERESTS

78.1 You are not allowed to undertake any external work or activity, paid or unpaid, that could be held to be in competition with, or in any way conflict with, the business interest of the Company.

78.2 If you wish to work in any other business, whether on a paid or voluntary basis, you must first obtain the written permission of the Company.

78.3 You should not have any financial interest in, or involvement with, any competing business or supplier other than via ownership of shares in companies listed on the Stock Exchange. If your family or friends are involved with competing businesses or supplier agreements where that involvement could be seen as a potential conflict of interest then you must inform the Company in writing. Failure to do so might result in disciplinary action.

78.4 Failure to disclose a potential conflict of interest will be considered a serious disciplinary offence that may be subject to summary dismissal.

79. CRIMINAL CONVICTIONS

79.1 You are required to inform the Company in writing of any Court cases in which you are involved which result in your criminal conviction. You must also tell the Company if you are listed on the Sex Offenders Register.

79.2 If you are arrested on suspicion of a criminal offence a full investigation will be undertaken as and when the Company deems appropriate. Disciplinary action, which may include dismissal, may be taken if the alleged offence and/or sentence have an impact on your work, or which destroys trust and confidence, causes the Company to lose confidence in your integrity, is unacceptable to other employees or has the potential to bring the Company into disrepute.

79.3 Failure to notify the Company of any of the above matters may result in disciplinary action being taken against you which could lead to a dismissal.

80. HOME WORKING

80.1 The Company recognises that home working can be beneficial to both employees and the Company. The Company reserves the right to ask you to work from home, or you may make a request to your line manager to work from home, for all or part of the working week.

80.2 Whilst not all jobs are suitable for home working, any request by you will be considered on its merits.

80.3 The employee's ability to request home working is not intended to create any contractual rights for staff over and above the statutory flexible working regime. A home working arrangement can be withdrawn or changed by the Company at any time without the agreement of the employee. But whenever possible and reasonable, withdrawal of a home working arrangement will be done in consultation with the employee and reasonable notice will be given, just as with any other proposed alteration to terms of employment.

80.4 Home working arrangements will usually be withdrawn if the effective and efficient operation of the team, department, and/or division is compromised, and/or:

80.4.1 the role changes;

80.4.2 the ability of the wider Company to fulfil its objectives is compromised;

80.4.3 the performance of a home worker is unsatisfactory; and/or

80.4.4 the Company has cause to believe that 'home working' is not 'going to plan' for whatever reason.

80.5 If home working is agreed, employees will have responsibility for ensuring they have a suitable environment at home in which they can focus on work.

80.6 The Company reserves the right to visit and inspect the employee's home working environment and facilities to check health and safety issues and that the home environment is suitable.

80.7 Home working must not put additional burden on office based colleagues, i.e. not lead to an output from the employee concerned which is reduced in either quality or quantity.

80.8 Employees are required to comply with all Company policies and procedures (eg. those relating to records management and the security of information) whether working at home or on Company premises.

81. NOTICE BOARDS / INTRANET

81.1 It is your duty to read all notices on the Company's notice boards, and to familiarise yourself with the Company's policies as published on the intranet from time to time and to comply with their requirements. Not knowing of any notice or policy will not generally be accepted as an excuse for non-compliance.

81.2 You should not place signs, bills or notices on the Company notice board without the prior written approval of your line manager.

81.3 You should not use the intranet for personal uses without the prior written approval of your line manager.

82. PRESS ENQUIRIES

All media enquiries should be referred to your line manager; no comments should be made, on or off the record, without prior reference and permission.

83. INTELLECTUAL PROPERTY

Any intellectual property created or produced by you during the course of your employment with the Company belongs to the Company and may not be used by you except in the performance of your duties or with the permission of the Company. Such work will remain the property of the Company and you must agree to assign the property rights to the Company, if requested.

84. RETIREMENT

The Company will not require employees to retire simply because of their age.

85. REFERENCES

85.1 The Company does not normally give a reference when an employee leaves other than a 'factual' reference. A factual reference simply states the dates of employment and job title.

85.2 The Company may give a reference which contains more information that a factual reference at its discretion.

86. 'OPEN DOOR' POLICY

The Company operates an 'open door' policy and you should never hesitate to raise with the Company any matter which worries you.

87. TRADE UNIONS

Whilst the Company does not have any formal association with any trade union it recognises that every employee has the right to decide to become a member of a trade union or similar association if they so wish.

88. RECOUPMENT RELATING TO ABSENCES

If your absence from work is due to negligence or damage caused by a third party and a claim is made in reference to that, we reserve the right to recover payments that we may have made to you as a result of the injury or absence.

89. CHANGES TO HANDBOOK

89.1 As stated in the Introduction, this Staff Handbook may be altered, deleted or added to by the Company as occasion requires or as legislation demands. Such legislative changes as are mandatory on the Company will be deemed to take effect on or before the effective date of the legislation. However, whenever practical and reasonable, the terms of any other proposed alteration or addition will be discussed as appropriate and/ or posted on the notice board and any Company intranet.

89.2 We hope that this Staff Handbook helps you to understand the way in which the Company works and your role within it. But please raise any matter you are not clear about with your line manager, or a senior member of management.

90. REDUNDANCY

The Company is committed to ensuring that if redundancies were to become necessary they would be kept to a minimum wherever possible. Our priority would be to find alternatives to redundancy. Please refer to the Company's Redundancy Policy if redundancies become relevant.